Our Vegetable Garden

Sally Cowan

Photographs by Lyz Turner-Clark

Contents

A Plan for the Garden   2

The Garden Shop   4

Making the Garden   6

Looking After the Garden   10

Good Vegetables   12

Glossary   16

A Plan for the Garden

We made a vegetable garden at my school.

We had to make a plan for the garden.

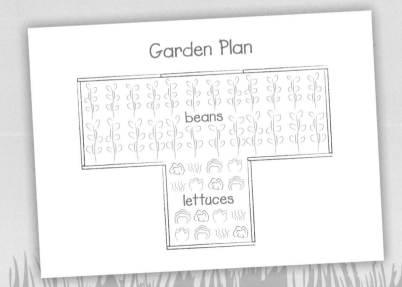

Garden Plan

beans

lettuces

The Garden Shop

Our teacher
went to a plant shop
to get vegetable seeds
for our garden.

He got vegetable plants, too.

Making the Garden

All the children helped
to make the vegetable garden.

We dug some **plant food**
into the garden beds.

I planted some bean seeds and some lettuce plants.

I got water for my plants.

We got some **mulch**
for the plants, too.

Looking After the Garden

All the children looked after the garden.

The plants got bigger and bigger.

Good Vegetables

Today we got
some vegetables
from our garden.

I got some lettuces.

We had some
of the vegetables
for our lunch.

Our vegetables
are very good!

Glossary

mulch

plant food